CW01346344

Sarah James

Darling Blue
[the lover I couldn't forget]

Indigo Dreams Publishing

First Edition: Darling Blue [the lover I couldn't forget]
First published in Great Britain in 2025 by:
Indigo Dreams Publishing
24, Forest Houses
Cookworthy Moor
Halwill
Beaworthy
Devon
EX21 5UU

www.indigodreamspublishing.com

ISBN 978-1-912876-97-6

British Library Cataloguing in Publication Data. A CIP record for this book can be obtained from the British Library.

Designed and typeset in Palatino Linotype by Indigo Dreams.
Cover design by Ronnie Goodyer.
Printed and bound in Great Britain by 4edge Ltd.

Papers used by Indigo Dreams are recyclable products made from wood grown in sustainable forests following the guidance of the Forest Stewardship Council.

For all those that paint the way
– the blues
& the deeper shades
which change the love we thought we knew

Acknowledgements

I'm extremely grateful to Dawn and Ronnie at Indigo Dreams for choosing Darling Blue as a winner of the Geoff Stevens Memorial Prize 2024 and for making the publication process so smooth and enjoyable.

My great thanks to the journal editors and competition judges who first recognised and published some of these poems (as listed below). Also, to Droitwich Writers' Circle, The Poetry Society's Worcestershire Stanza and poetry buddies Jenna, Dave and Sue for their feedback on draft poems. Gratitude too to Matthew M.C. Smith whose feedback on an earlier ekphrastic poetry pamphlet version led to me including QR codes for viewing the artworks and to the narrator's personal story interwoven between the ekphrastic poems.

Finally, my thanks to those who look after the artworks and allow the public to enjoy them, including Tate Britain, Lady Lever Art Gallery in Port Sunlight, Manchester Art Gallery, Oxford's Ashmolean Museum and Birmingham Museum and Art Gallery.

Previous recognition/publication of versions of these poems include: Darling Blue in *The Lake;* Bluebell Blue (joint runner-up in the Pre-Raphaelite Society Poetry Competition 2023) in *PRS Review;* The Skyscraper in *The Fruits of Starmer's Labour: The Bread & Roses Poetry Award Anthology 2023* (Culture Matters, 2023); This Flood (the Chair's Commendation in the Pre-Raphaelite Society Poetry Competition 2022) in *PRS Review;* A touch of watercolour in *The Lake;* The River Girl in *iamb;* Love's Slow Art (commended in the These 3 Streams Poetry Competition 2022); Owerblawing in *Black Bough Poetry Christmas & Winter Anthology Volume 5,* and a poetryfilm version in the *Wirral Poetry Festival Poetry Video Anthology 2024.*

A short note on reading the poems

Ekphrastic pieces have QR codes, which may be scanned to view the artworks online. These poems are in Baskerville Old Face font.

Poems featuring the fictional narrator's life-story are in Palatino Linotype font, though there is intentional crossover content between the ekphrastic and narrative pieces.

CONTENTS

Darling Blue

[the lover I couldn't forget]

One of Neptune's Horses Drinks from the Sea of Dreams

after 'Neptune's Horses' by Walter Crane

The white storm of my eyes is clouded by miles,
by hours in relentless waves, pounding out miles.

My mane and tail are unending swirls of spray,
swallowing years and lives for thousands of miles.

Which shore I first came from lost even to me,
my place, my home, is only now's tallied miles.

Each crescent moon left by my webbed hooves' thundering
heralds a sky-wide soul, unbounded by miles.

Try to ride me, I dare you, if you believe
you could bridle my will or hound down these miles.

You'll never come close; no one will ever tame
or break this Neptune Horse confounding the miles.

Your Fingers

At the hotel room, pressing your key card
to the door, pushing open my heart.

A gasp or two later, clicking off light
and noise, turning on fires inside.

Tracing my lips like the brimming rim
of a wine glass learning how to sing.

Cat's-cradling my head afterwards while
I drink the bright sky from your eyes.

It takes hours for my breath to shrink
back to the size of your finger-tip;

I almost believe this moment could last
as long as my life, outrunning our pasts.

Then your fingers wake once more,
to tap-dance on your phone and reach for

the remote.

Darling Blue
after 'The Little Speedwell's Darling Blue' by John Everett Millais

The only hints of blue are touches of sky
on the distant mountains and two sprigs
of bird's-eye speedwell in the child's hand
and lap, vivid against her white dress,
like the black shoe peeping out beneath its hem.

The ground she's sitting on is as hazy
as the sky and mountain, except for a few spikes
of grass and the growing heap of picked flowers
at her side: ox-eyed daisies, dog roses, pink
fragments of something unidentifiable

and the yellow of what might be cat's-ear, rough
hawkbit, cornfield marigold, or even the petals
of grounded stars. The speedwell she holds closest
might have been intended as hope of spring
but my eyes mistake it for forget-me-not,

a cry for what is lost reminding us
how little remains. Impossible to tell if her gaze
is dreamy, simply that it's downcast, the sad heap
of petals beside her still growing. How long
will she keep on picking? Beyond

her own death now she's painted into infinity.
I'm sure only I see this pile as prescient
of a world with nothing left to pick.
But what of the children I might want
to have, my grandkids and their futures?

The heap of picked flowers slowly wilts
into the blur of changing seasons.

Closed Book, Open Painting

Meeting in galleries, lectures or talks, we share the passion that will keep our secret safe, or so we hope. Every loving glance at a piece of art is a coded message, though precise meanings are difficult to decipher. The light kiss of artists' brush-tips to their painting's skin, the liquid flow caressing the canvas, the pouring out of souls...and that tangling of intentions and understanding which eventually follows. What does any 'we' signify when it's all read between the lines, relying on personal interpretation of symbolic significance, magic inference and metaphors that may later turn out to be more context-specific than they seemed at the time? I guess this is how he wanted things – exciting enough to light sparks, yet contained enough to return home to his wife. What I wanted has never really come into it. If it had, my choice would probably still have been him, though it's tricky to say for sure when already passed the point of strangers. Once love has a face and shape known by heart, sometimes, the only way on, or out, is getting to know them better.

That Sleeve
after 'The Sisters' by James Collinson

Don't imagine I'd be the most striking
of the two – even I can't decide which
is best: golden ringlets or ebony curls,
to be the older one 'who should act their age'
or the younger, forever treated like a baby.

Don't be fooled by our half-
smiles, lips curving around what's unsaid:
that she gets a warm shawl, red poppies
on her head and a white dog rose
to hold, while I simply get a red ribbon
and may only hug her presence –
in an embrace shaped by the need
to restrain her from lashing out
or clamping my shoulders too tightly.

Don't question her crowning garland
or the scattering of leaves she's been given
to decorate the edge of her shawl.
Although some are still green, the rest
are as dead as her autumn hair
flustered by the wind, while her cloak
now seems more comfort-blanket material
than Little Miss Red Riding Hood.

Don't let others label it love, or mistake
it for hate. Our mirrored expressions are both
at the same time. If I could release myself
from this pose and scratch her face,
I wouldn't hesitate: my nails
are sharper than hedgerow thorns.

Sisters, yet the isolation of an only child
flung together with all the other only/lonely
kids to see who sticks first... If it comes
to a fight with my rival/sibling, don't doubt
that I could win. See how easily the lace
is draping away from this arm, where years
of hidden tricks I've had to learn
may be pulled discretely from that sleeve,
the sleeve used earlier to wipe my nose.

Ready? Watch my eyes slowly fill with tears.

Dear Blue (1)

This seems the most obvious secret name
to give you: the colour of your eyes,
the shade that strikes you in art,
and the widest range of hues I come across,
then find a smile
on my face as I'm reminded of you.

But a name is not enough;
I've no idea what to do
with all the love notes I can't send,
the caring that can't be reduced
to a work text or shared
in an erasable snatched chat.

Most of my world
has become virtual:
time stretched thin between
the rare flames of feeling
really alive –
tingling, touching, tasting…

When I die, the sum
of my life won't be my bones,
a few etched clichés on a tombstone
or a brief outpouring on social media.
It will be the invisible braille
of your lips on my skin.

And when someone says "blue",
they won't even know it's an elegy for me
talking/not-talking to you.

Bluebell Blue
after 'April Love' by Arthur Hughes

In this painted pose, everything
except for her hair, face and arm
is the blue of a spring flower.
As if he'd picked the stem of her,
then let the dress shape a bell
around this green heart, drawing

up from the earth and turning
towards the sun. Only, her eyes
remain downcast, gazing into
the space of absence beside her.
The firm tree trunk at her back
is a tangled web of clinging ivy

and shadow, leaves twisting away
from their own heart shapes. Parted,
her lips open without budding.
The fabric flow of her skirt's silent
petalled bell is an un-swimmable ocean.
When she steps out of this scene,

this love, will she take her scarf
with her, clasped close as a dream?
Perhaps she will let it drop instead,
leaving its soft curves of sky and river
to soak up more rain, another scrap of blue
slowly drowned by the weight of mud.

Your Lips

Their two crescent moons bob together
on an ocean of dreams while you sleep,
sailing towards and away from me.

I watch, trying not to wonder what
or who has you smiling like this.

That smile becomes a coiled spring
when tensed for your lectures, or a frayed rope
for small talk, ends twitching in polite flickers.

I've no inkling what they look like
while kissing, only the sensation

of openness swallowing me in, my heart
matching the pulse of your tongue,
the taste of tonic mixing with gin.

I've no idea how they are when locked
with your wife's, or chatting to family.

A man known without knowing his kin
is more than partly still a stranger.
I only have a fraction of your smiles,

not those you were born with, or return
home to. Our half-smiles meet as if

to complete each other, without a clue
of how much more is missing.

Too Much to Swallow

after 'The Beguiling of Merlin' by Edward Burne-Jones

Merlin believes his neck may now be cricked
forever at an awkward angle, his face crooked,
as he finds himself transfixed by Nimue's gaze,
pinned by the butterflying pages in her hand.

She should be holding the book in a way
that signifies women have lots lacking, lots they need
to learn, not flicking as if her mind will never
be satisfied with such limited knowledge.

This heavy text is close to flying, as if nothing left
to teach her. The hawthorn where he's sitting
has weaved itself into a cage without bars, an 'O!'
of bewitchment from which he can't break free.

The tree's alive with the white blossom of her spell
made visible. By her bare feet, a cluster of Siberian irises
rise up like hungry cobras with open mouths; more
of their piercing blue tongues are pushing through

the hawthorn's snowdrift. Merlin's flesh is melting
wax loosening from bone, while her stare feels
like a livid bruise. His shoes are pinching, shape-
shifting into women's sandals, his jaw softening –

even his thoughts no longer seem his own.
Instead of slate slowly chipped away, the fabric
of Nimue's almost see-through dress is slipping
from ripples of grey to torrents of river blue

pouring down her curves in a waterfall
that's gaining force. He's no longer sure
the timid blue flowers that turned serpentine
weren't once as white as the blossom crying out

beneath him, until she magicked their petals
to the colour of summer sky, the tone too of a shoreless
ocean beyond his control. The hawthorn’s slithering
branches snake around him, constricting.

Merlin's eyes marble. His arm droops
as his scarf and tunic tighten, their dark green
taking on a deeper blue than he’s ever seen;
breath wilts on his lips.

Questions

Most artists slept with their models. He declares this in a matter-of-fact tone, as if it were as much part of painting as how to best mix watercolours, build up layers or cover over small slips. My memory may be unfair; it's possible he said 'many', not 'most'. I try not to imagine how this would have been, glad he isn't an artist and that I'm not a model to be set in any pose he chooses. Except, maybe this is what we are, only, with different words to describe our roles. Would I have fallen for him if he'd told me from the start not just that he was married, but married and seemingly happily? Or is this what keeps us going – the fleeting glimpse of something other powering through our everyday mundanity? Still, he's created a version of myself that I both love and hate, and it's that I can't forgive, even as I dance for him in the red silk shoes he's Hans-Christian-Andersened from my heart.[1] In any relationship, there is a leader and the led, but the led must allow themselves to follow.[2] So many kinds of influence, so many types of following, while emotion and reason waltz to different tunes.[3] In my head now, at least, I make him my muse instead.

[1] *Is drawing on fairytale rather than myth, an alternative / innovation, a small act of artistic defiance or just / another return to allusive/elusive rendering?*
[2] *And what about those / that alternate / between both of them?*
[3] *Do all artists simply make use / of whatever's available?*

In the Moment

after 'Cloister Lilies' by Marie Spartali Stillman

I could fall in love with her youth and beauty,
have fallen into the daydream of her gaze –
her eyes are warm wood which could be
kindled to flame, but not a votive candle.

The white lilies in her hand won't focus her.
Nor the weight of prophetic lilies at her shoulders.
The rosary beads looped to her other wrist
are pulling away from the bright pictures

and blurred scripture in her prayer book.
Yellowed; they look like false pearls.
Her braided hair is as golden as the trim
of her blue top and the lilies' pollened stamen.

The rest of her long locks cascade free...
suppose the streaks in her blue clothes aren't folds
in the fabric, or sun playing across the billowing
pinched in by gold brocade, but a thinning of belief.

Poking through, darker sleeves fitted more tightly
to her lower arms, hiding what lies beneath, quietening
bare flesh and shivers. Florence is a hot smudge
of buildings behind her, all the trees narrowed

to densely packed needles, letting only ghosts
of light through. Out of sight, two trilling rock doves,
twining grapevines, the scent of peeled oranges... Hard
to say if it's hay fever or fear of sacred vows brimming

in her eyes. Pray to God, she doesn't sneeze
and break this moment's daydream.

The Skyscraper

I'm in the basement bar of a glass Eiffel Tower, twisting
the cocktail in my hand. A champagne coupe of sparklers:
the half-a-passion-fruit boat on top filled with spirit
and powder, then set alight: a small blaze on night's ocean.

This drink's £20 a time, but that's alright: he's buying,
his fingers stroking mine while I sink one, two, three...
they taste like decadence, slip down way too easily –
as easily as the thin strap of my slinky top

slips from my shoulder, while the ground sways away
from my feet. Up in his room, the city below is a glitter
of twinkling lights unravelled from a giant Christmas tree.
I am the present, being slowly unwrapped.

I don't know who I am at this moment, nor the man
at my side. Suspended here like an exclamation mark
that doesn't have to fall towards a full stop, I curve into
the wild escape of it. A ghost of me in the glass smiles back.

Afterwards, I re-wrap my softness into the anonymity
of a fluffy white towelling robe, its fresh laundered warmth.
Only later, do I think of the hundred other bodies
that have worn it before, with just a quick mechanical rinse

and spin in between. A gift tag is not a price tag,
I tell myself, as the elevator speeds downwards
and I slip from the shiny glass out into a frosty dawn.
Like Christmas, I want to pretend I still believe this.

The Day Dreams

after Dante Gabriel Rossetti

	What Jane[1] might come to find
to read or design fades	in importance beside
the fragile bindweed[6] -	open-mouthed white[0] petals,
a lone heart-shaped leaf -	rested in one hand on her
wordless pages.	Every detail's a hint of
hope, a dream made	half-real[4]. Willow is the frame
she'll blossom free	with, though its gentle branches
will later cede	to sycamore[7], Gabriel's first
bloom traded[5]	for honeysuckle. Dream's lost
love-rich longing	can't bear full-season
intensity; swapping	from chalk and light pastels
to thick oils calls for	bolder brushstrokes, sharpened
colours. It pays well -	as his last finished painting,
its worth[3] will swell	- but this earlier drawing[2] haunts
my heart more.	

[0]Flowering Footnotes

[1] model or maker, maker or muse -
[2] which does he rate higher?
[3] and how does he value them/her?
[4] what if life is never any other than this?
[5] to barter or not to barter - an artist's dilemma
[6] worth nothing more than what suits the wider picture
[7] or the frame it's placed in

Object(ive) Evaluation

If I were a painting, would he cut me from my frame? What then – roll me up and slip me into his jacket alongside his wallet, next to the sharp plastic edge of his debit cards? His outer pocket's linen hanky smells of home – the lavender scent of a different washing powder to my own. I know because I borrowed it last week to breathe in this impression of lazy summer heat, then try to hold onto it. Now the sense of freshness has gone, all that's left is the loud buzzing of bees bumbling through blossom, drowsy-headed and heavy with sticky pollen.

If they looked more closely
after 'Juliet/The Blue Necklace' by John William Waterhouse

Already, they're trying to make a ghost
of me – the bright red dress of my blood
and womanhood glazed in a mist of white fabric
that subdues everything constrained below.

Even my blue necklace must be clutched
and fingered. Like a rosary, beads of sky
or river solidified, instead of flowing onwards.

They will suppose I'm dreaming of my one
and only Romeo, a man I'd happily die for.

But it's not love-sick anxiety that fidgets me,
rather a mulling over of alternatives
which might be easier than the slow death

of romance and marriage. Even the pink walls,
smudged here to a virginal blush, are scratched
with a longing to break away. If they looked
more closely at my sealed lips, they'd see

this redness is unquenchable.

Dear Blue (2)

I almost left you again last week.
Packing to go home to my parents alone
for Christmas, I screamed
into my suitcase,
then sat on the bed, staring
at my phone.

One call,
one message, is all
it should take.
Except, who would I be phoning
or texting?

An empty drawer in the garage,
a hidden compartment in your car,
where you stash
the mobile you only use for one purpose.

Three days is too long
to go unanswered,
and yet still I hang around
for your call.

I almost left you last week;
it will happen again for sure.

This Flood
after 'A Flood' by John Everett Millais

Almost out of frame, a goldfinch waits, beak closed
to song. Along the bare branches, sparkling raindrops
wait too, ready to drip – onto the street now turned
to muddy river. Another flustered bird is mid-flight.

The lone baby in a cradle floating below isn't Moses.
The witch-black kitten keeping guard on top of the ruffled
quilt is a rough-furred, open-mouthed hiss and spit
of snarls. Beside them, a jug slowly sinks into the sludge.

This child's cloudless eyes are transfixed by something
above, beyond our sight, though it could be the quiver
of the infant's own out-stretched fingers, unable yet
to grasp shadows and light, movement or meaning.

No, the newborn's wide-open lips aren't haloing around
a silent 'oh'. If the cradle is an ark, it's for the startled cat
not the adrift baby. The distant punt that's racing
this cargo's weight can't push towards them fast enough.

Balanced on its branch, the watching songbird's beak
is closed to any sound – help isn't coming, today or at all.

The bits we do/don't leave behind

The hotel rooms that used to cocoon us are dead silkworms – no spinning left in them. My red dancing shoes have worn themselves out. Every place where he's told me to slip off these heels and entwine my legs with his has an invisible patch of threadbare carpet. Frayed patterns mark other worn spots where he's cupped my Cinderella-glass soles in his hands, before removing them to run his palms up my calves, then thighs.

his size ten brogue
under the bed, lace dangling –
a loose mooring rope

He's never let me give him anything except memories and a promise that we'll see each other soon. Every time we part, he gives me a new print – a postcard copy of one of the paintings we've seen. Back in my flat, I tack them up, positioning each with care to create my own small gallery. A collage of our time together, without us in it.

a postcard-size gap
between prints frames a landscape
of bare wall

I know he's not quite cruel or thoughtless enough to take the exact same postcards home to his wife. But would it matter now if he did?

Neptune's Horse Dances
after 'Neptune's Horses' by Walter Crane

The white of my eyes is a measure of miles,
relentless tides and storms raging on for miles.

My mane and tail are endless cascades of spray,
swallowing years and lives, tumbling windswept miles.

Each wild crescent moon marked by the thundering hooves
of my sky-wide soul charts more than time and miles.

Try to ride me, I dare you, if you believe
any bridle could control me or these miles.

You'll never come close; no one will ever tame
or break this Neptune Horse outracing all miles.

Fabrication

I didn't know it at the time, but I lied too, not for him but to him. It turns out I never wanted him to leave her; I just wanted something to change, something to make him loosen his grip on me. Of course, it was up to me to break free, to re-work this ill-conceived picture and create a meaningful palimpsest without effacing myself in the process. I failed.

Inevitability
after 'The Days of Creation: The First Day' by Edward Burne-Jones

Imagine dressing in a long cloak of crow
and dove feathers inseparably intermingled,
but keeping life not death hidden beneath.
This is the moment where free will is more
than an illusion, fate still undecided,
though light and darkness may already

be splitting apart in the crystal ball that will
become your Earth. This angel has no smile,
no answers, only the heavy globe balanced
in her hands and a shadowy feather/serpent's head
resting on her hair. Even her opalescent wings
have been folded away for her, their silk

impossible to fly with, the wet ground too slippery
to walk far. The only part of her reflected there
is her feet: nails clipped to small moons, their flesh
a manly clay set firm now to angel bones. Against
the creator's wishes, I prise this piece from the rest
of his work as if plucking out a feather.

White or black, her plumage isn't one of lacking;
the tones of both dove and crow mark
their borders with blues of sky and ocean.
The sphere she's holding shines like a lake
of liquid potential too large for one lonely being
to keep steady without spilling a single drop

of life. Imagine waking up every morning
still trying to get past that first day –
or the relationship that shaped you, the one
you'd break the whole world to escape from.

'Me', c. 2020, Anon

Leave enough blank space, life will rush to fill it. No need to frame and hang this. Years pass. Light and laughter brushstroke over.

Not Mourning

after 'Gone, But Not Forgotten' by John William Waterhouse

The stone is the same tone as her flesh,
though no way of knowing if this is for
the process of her immortalisation as a statue,
or because her warm touch alone is enough
to give light to this graveyard tomb
or memorial draped with roses.

The background sky and trees are as fuzzy
as a memory from long ago, making the precise
brushstrokes of her face, her body and the leaves
illuminated by her presence more striking.

I want her thoughts though, the how
and why of the way she holds her spray
of picked flowers as if she's forgotten
they're in her hand, now drooping back
towards the ground. Is there mystery,
mourning, or simply tiredness
in her down-turned gaze?

My eye's drawn to the bottom corner's
red spillage that could be rags, or fabric
discarded in a rush. Whatever's been left or not
left, a fleshy bloom scratches at her neck
like a clumsy hand itching after something lost.

I lift my fingers absent-mindedly
to my own face in search of what's missing –
the smoothness of a budding complexion,
the stubborn jut of a determined chin,
sure of where it's heading...

Perhaps, like me, she has just slipped out
of another life, and, instead of carrying this
with her, has chosen to leave her younger self
in a place where it can do no harm,
while the flowers strung across the stone wall
have grown from the thread of those stitches
she had to unpick to get free.

There may be mourning, but,
by her head, a loosely tied blue ribbon
flutters with new meaning.

Dear Blue (3)

It's strange how even now
I still write love notes to you
in my mind, though the few
I sent then were for instant click,
read, delete. Nothing kept
outside your head, nothing allowed
that might be seen
and understood by others.

If I said that this note is different:
a habit I can't unlearn more than
a caring which still exists…

Something my younger self trapped
emerges occasionally
from my memory's labyrinth of twists
and turns. I am no longer her,
and yet, part of her is still me.

And the love she brought to life
has become a separate living entity:
another minotaur which refuses to die,
guarding this maze like its own home,
trying to make the walls unscaleable,
creating a temple to its own existence.

Traces linger, regardless.

A touch of watercolour
after 'Apse of the Duomo, Pisa' by John Ruskin

I see a ghost of the cathedral
from the outside: its pillars, arches
and mosaic details seeping colour
and wisping away at the edges
back to a daydream of white paper.

Textured by sun, it's as if warm light
has softened the building, melted
a fragment of it to the page. Shadows
zoetrope the columns and curves
of the mid-layer of colonnades.

Like this, the structure is more
beautiful: unfinished, as ephemeral
as a wedding cake first taking shape
in a lover's mind. Or a birdcage
in marble, rendered only in part

to set the soul free – still whole,
its delicacy intricate and intact.
The artist's touch of watercolour
and brush might be gentler than a kiss,
more tender than any caress,

but this drawing's elusive dream
will last longer than a lover's heart
or any faith built from stone.

Negative Space

There is an art to piecing someone back together. I started with my setting. Deleting his number from my phone, packaging up all his postcards, then re-decorating my flat, passing on any work where we might meet. Not quite cold turkey, but near enough. Erasing his touch, the unexpected reminders, those memories that keep trying to rewrite themselves...this is harder. Every day I have to tell myself who I am now, chant a mantra of successful unattached single woman. I pedestal my professional role of the exhibition organiser everyone wants to hire. That nearly everyone does hire, except him. It's like dressing a model for a painting. Only both the model and artist are me, and I've no intention of keeping still. Slowly, I learn how to recognise the positive space of my own body outside the context of his absence.

Flickering
after 'The Ponte Vecchio, Florence' by William Holman Hunt

Florence isn't Venice but the quiet sparkle
and watery ripples of this city scene at night
take me straight back to our Venetian escape.

I've only visited the place once, and this return
through my memories is not like then's love-glazed,
hand-in-hand break from reality, living briefly

in a summer dream set far-away from everyday.
I gaze at the actual painted scene - set elsewhere
in Italy - during a British winter of minus two outside.

My lone staring takes in its lit bridge and stone
structures, glistening even brighter in the river's
reflective flow than through the taper-slit windows

built up from solid foundations on the Arno's banks,
braced no doubt by firm ground, perhaps hard rock.
In those days, I guess this radiance would have been

candles, maybe even a wish list of shining lights,
kept aflame by Vatican-like faith and devotion.
My love burns differently. I pull my home and life

around me and snuggle into the warmth, right here,
right now. A print of this painting on the lounge wall
will fit nicely over the flickering shadows.

Dear Blue (4)

Now I no longer write to you, I can't decide
whether to write instead to my new love
or to a reader who'll never
come across these words.

Is it wrong to most want
to write love letters to a stranger,
to talk to someone who'll never know me
or let me down?
To ask if any love can last
that long or safely run that far ahead?

The romance of a passion that spans centuries…

If the future happened on these notes to you,
would they imagine Blue as a man
or woman? Would they understand
how different, yet how the same,
this love is to their own?

A citrus scent merged with pine trees,
or the smoothness of leaf or paint mixed
with the roughness of bark or canvas.
A taste on the tongue that's sweat and sex.
Shadow silhouettes on the walls
and curtains that move as one.

All this and something else
entirely individual, like
the way in which a past love
later lives on within another.

If you met my new man,
you would not like him.

The River Girl

after 'The Lady of Shalott' by John William Waterhouse

Maybe her real curse is Lancelot himself, glimpsed
unwillingly. The glass in her mirror shatters
like a Cinderella slipper forced onto the wrong foot.
Or so the myth goes... She steps into her boat
in a dress of innocence that's bridal white.

Sitting upright, her gaze is alive, but eyes fixed
on something out of sight. She has no oars
or means of steering, only her arms outstretched
slightly at her sides like swan-wings half-prepared
to fly or glide. Except, she doesn't move;

she's as still as a dead Viking on a funeral pyre
about to be lit and set adrift. As yet, the only flames
are a lantern at the golden prow and one taper candle,
another two having blown to smoke. But her hair
is ready to set fire to the autumn trees in a slow blaze

across this whole landscape. Her tapestried quilt
drapes in the water. Already, a layer of colour
from the tales patterned by that fabric
has slipped onto the river's surface, like a dream
which has lost both shape and meaning but not

its fluidity. If she were to dive in now to swim
for shore, she'd arrive with a new life dyed
into the white of her clinging dress – dripping
weed, yes, but also the taste of fresh flowing rain
and how brightly sunlight shines through

when freed from a cracked mirror.

Love's Slow Art

I love to watch him work. He pairs leaves,
skeletonned by autumn's dancing red fall,
with feathers gifted by the wind and dark clouds.

He takes storm-battered remnants, beached up
miles away from home, and transforms
their curves into more than driftwood art.

His eye close as a kissing lip, his fingers stroke
and smooth surfaces rubbed raw by rough weather.
He breathes light into each husk nestled in his palm.

Tending to those still living is harder.
He feeds and waters grounded fledglings for days
before relinquishing them to the sky's wideness.

It took me years of watching and waiting
to trust that such broken things, even me,
might be coaxed by him to shine again.

Despite his own past, his own pains, sharing
the brightness of others' lives with gentle smiles.
We listen together through sleepless hours

for dawn-winged song.

Unstoppable
after 'Autumn Leaves' by John Everett Millais

The girls in Millais's painting don't know
what they're doing: heaping leaves for him
into a pile ready to fuel an autumn pyre.

Nature's beauty won't be burnt so easily.
All it takes is for a single stray leaf to blow free

and cartwheel, fire-red, across the grass,
out of the garden and down the street, as far
away as it can reach before it's grounded.

Earth settles; seasons pass, until it's time
for another tree, another leaf, with no memory

of all the leaves that have been and gone,
or the similar scenes lived already by others,
though framed by their own viewpoint.

Here I am now, two centuries later, staring
at a new canvas unfolding before my eyes.

Light matchstick-strikes everything: the red
in my son's hair, the red of the waterfall's
muddy rush and tumble, the autumn glow

to the trees, slowly releasing their grip
on the year's last torrent of copper and gold.

My son perches on a boulder, briefly
as stilled as Millais's Ophelia. But, below
the surface, his currents tug: a smile eddies

at the corners of his lips; the river gushes
through not over him, unstoppable in its flow

onwards. I zoom in on the sycamore's raft
of red, each grounded leaf palming rain
just as lily pads palm petals on still water.

Inside each pellet of liquid reflections, a forest
of floating leaves and my face, peering closer –

as I do in galleries, seeking the source
of inspiration for oils now placed behind glass
and framed with dead wood, not the life

within nature and our shifting seasons. I turn
back to my son, lit bright as a candle flame.

His eyes sparkle like paused raindrops;
within them, they too hold whole worlds
which haven't yet been painted.

A father

stacks up blocks ten times in a row
to be knocked down ten times in an instant;

wipes noses and tears, mud and blood;

holds hands or a sick bowl, ready
to steady any heaving, wobble or tilt;

changes clothes and sheets, scrubs vomit
from nooks and lattices no one else notices;

ties laces, smooths collars, straightens ties;

bones up on history he never wanted
to know so he can help with homework;

feels every growing pain, then grows faster
to keep up with his son's needs, and settle

the fears that come with loving;

teaches his son more than he knows
that he knows.

Before something burns or bursts
after 'Priestess of Delphi' by John Collier

She's about to catch alight – a blood-rush blaze
of bright red cloth in place of flowing hair,
more molten red fabric flickering on her lap,
folding and flaming deep with shadows.

Her eyes are closed, body leaning lightly
into her trance without falling from the tall
gold-clawed stool, where she's perched
like a clipped songbird with nothing to grab

to prevent toppling. Her dress is almost
one in colour with the sides of her seat
and the ground below, cracked like a walnut,
releasing pulses of smoke and steam.

In her left hand, a sprig of laurel, alert
as an aerial to tune in with. Or a wick
to burn from. Beneath her feet, heated
by the swirls of gas escaping from the earth,

a twist of something like bay leaves
roasted to a golden-brown crispness,
while the bowl in her other hand
is as good as empty. No ice to cool her

from her trance, though her dress's spots
could be small flowers, smudged hearts
or a red star-chart with a join-the-dot guide
to surviving the prophecy playing out

on the movie-screen of her shut eyelids.
She doesn't seem scared or happy,
simply enraptured, delaying the moment
when she'll burst into flame or have to let

reality back in, the mystery of her dream
seeping away like the red material slipping
from her knees... Left on myth's canvas
like that, she's still suspended in all

possible futures, including those
no one wants to see.

Restoration

Maybe what I loved most then was the added intensity of a shared passion. It's easy to forget that collectors tend to stick with what they know. Familiarity can soon lead to a sense of disappointment, and a greed for something new, until that too loses its novelty. The real test of time, and so much else besides, is to step away and see how you feel about the same piece when you return to it. Catching the eye anew, shapes and colours may strike again as strongly. Or disillusion bite, recognising that it's not quite as bright or startling as the mind remembers.

Restoration may be possible, fading colours revitalised. But a painting never entirely regains its original state. There is a thrill to the process – a glimpse, perhaps, of the artist's signature, or another detail usually obscured by the frame or a build-up of grime. True new discoveries are rare, though small revelations may be marketed to the world as secrets painstakingly uncovered by this expensive bit-by-bit work. The delight of seeing something that was once hidden never lasts. Then comes the decision – to keep it regardless or auction it off to the highest bidder. I'd firmly advise the latter. Some loves can live on, undamaged, beyond their initial context, but it takes more than just a shared passion.

Owerblawing

after 'The Shortening Winter's Day is Near a Close' by Joseph/David Farquharson

Where it's hung now, this painting becomes
a palimpsest blur of gallery ghosts – the glass's
fragmented reflections of old building, lights
and other pictures overlay the white snow,
intricate sheep, spectral wood and shadowed tree.

Only the setting sun shines through this
interference. It's enough though that I want
to see more, enough for me to believe
that all I need to do is step through the frame
into the field and I'll feel the snow crackle
beneath my feet, a cold sparkle on my face...
everything around a glow of quiet peace.

Even the shepherd struggling with his straw bale
is about to lay it down, ready for the birth
of tomorrow's wonderful new day –
I can taste the icy sharpness, fresh snowfall
owerblawing the gallery's wooden floor.

His Heart

Unlike before, I don't ask for proofs of life:
I don't need to see it to believe its existence.

It's the warmth in his body and fingers,
always hotter than my own, giving heat to me.

It's his mist breath on frosty mornings,
patterning the air, entwining with mine.

It's the strong rhythmic beat, calming
troubled sleep or drumming over nightmares
with a tender music which dreams can settle into.

When I place my head on his chest and listen,
it's: the steady axe-stroke chopping clear our path;
the spade clunk digging firm foundations,
setting up boundary fences we've agreed on,
or shovelling snow from the doors.

I know already what his heart would look like
if I could see it – no quietly sculpted artistic marble
but a bloody red mess of throbbing muscle

keeping everything going.

More Than Neptune's Horse
after 'Neptune's Horses' by Walter Crane

The whites of my eyes light beyond measured miles,
breaching relentless rock and retreating shorelines.

Each crescent moon grooved by my thundering hooves
is brimful with wild dreams and soul-charted skies.

My mane and tail are vast crescendos of surf,
years of new horizons outracing past tides.

Try to ride me if you dare, if you think
any bridle could restrain or control me.

You will never come close; no one
will tame or break my spirit –

it haunts all you'll ever see or touch.

My last unsent letter

The ring you never gave me shines
more brightly on my finger placed there by him
beside a gold band that can't be broken.

For years, I refused to look at any pictures
you'd loved, in fear I'd catch light again,
a kindling which would never burn itself out.

I still carry a small flame of you with me,
but in a love that's as solid as it is molten,
taking on all the shapes and forms asked of it,

even the ones which may always lie
beyond you. Blue now is the summer sky
that he and I live, laugh and love under,

the still lake we walk around,
the sea which breaks from crashing waves
into surf-angels on sunlit shores.

Up close, this blue isn't a liquid anyone
can drink but distance's illusion – it trickles
colourlessly through clasped fingers,

falling away more silkily than a dress-
strap from my shoulder, or a brushstroke
of clear varnish, across a flaking canvas

already forgotten by its creator
in the search for a blue so intense
it can only ever grow deeper.

Extra notes for the ekphrastic poems

This collection draws on only a very small selection from the Pre-Raphaelite Brotherhood's art and influence. The poems shouldn't be taken as representative of the movement as a whole; they simply reflect some art that has inspired me. Likewise, these notes are a Pre-Raphaelite-art-lover's, rather than an expert's, and come with apologies for any errors in my research. For some pieces, especially where little information was readily available, the potential significances, symbolism and meanings drawn are my own.

One of Neptune's Horses Drinks from the Sea of Dreams (**Neptune's Horse Dances** and **More Than Neptune's Horse**): 'Neptune's Horses' by Walter Crane (1845-1915) was inspired by surf on an 1892 trip to America. He created several colour schemes in tempera and oil, exhibiting the first in the winter of 1892-93. His work is considered to span several artistic movements, styles and influences, including Pre-Raphaelite. The ghazal form used for part of my sequence, like the use of repetition with change across all three parts, reflects the fact that the horses themselves are a repetitive element (with small differences) in this artwork. The free verse version might be read as a breaking free from the painting, Neptune's control, a storm-struck past…

Darling Blue: 'The Little Speedwell's Darling Blue' (an oil on canvas, 1891-92) by John Everett Millais (1829-96) takes its title from Tennyson's 'In Memoriam', Section LXXXIII, which voices a longing for spring, with speedwell being one of the earliest wildflowers to open after winter. The child in the painting is Millais's granddaughter, Phyllis.

That Sleeve: 'The Sisters' is a c. 1860 oil painting by James Collinson (1825-1881), one of four invited members that joined the three initial Pre-Raphaelite Brotherhood founding members.

Bluebell Blue: 'April Love' (1855–6) by Arthur Hughes (1832-1915) was originally accompanied by an extract from Tennyson's 'The Miller's Daughter'. Although the painting features young lovers at a moment of emotional crisis, the male figure is barely visible. By contrast, the woman's sadness and the vivid blue of her clothing are hauntingly striking. Bluebells have six petals and the stanzas of my poem are each six lines.

Too Much to Swallow: 'The Beguiling of Merlin' by Edward Burne-Jones (1833-98) dates from 1873-77 and has a spell-binding presence.

In the Moment: 'Cloister Lilies' by Marie Spartali Stillman (1844-1927) was painted in 1891. She originally worked with the Pre-Raphaelites as a model but then trained and became a respected painter herself, living in Florence and Rome.

The Day Dreams: This poem is primarily inspired by Dante Gabriel Rossetti's 1872-8 pastel and black chalk on tinted paper 'The Day Dream'. It draws too on the relationship Rossetti (1828-82) had with his model, Jane Morris, and his subsequent 1879-80 oil on canvas. My poem acknowledges his own sonnet for the painting by using a mid-line abbaabbaccdeed slant-rhyme pattern within a contemporary structure.

If they looked more closely: 'Juliet/The Blue Necklace' is an 1898 oil on canvas by John William Waterhouse (1849-1917), featuring the Juliet of William Shakespeare's *Romeo and Juliet*.

This Flood: The 1870 oil on canvas 'A Flood' by John Everett Millais (1829-96) is said to have been most immediately inspired by an 1864 flood in Sheffield, where local newspapers reported that a child had been washed away in a cradle.

Inevitability: Edward Burne-Jones (1833-98) created a sequence of six pictures depicting 'The Days of Creation' (1870-76). Composed with watercolour, gouache, shell gold, and platinum paint on linen-covered panel prepared with zinc white ground, the artist wanted each piece to be viewed in the context of the rest, not on its own, and within the frame he designed for them. However, 'The First Day' appeals to me more than the others.

Not Mourning: 'Gone, But Not Forgotten' is an enigmatic 1873 painting by John William Waterhouse (1849-1917).

A touch of watercolour: 'Apse of the Duomo, Pisa' is an 1872 watercolour and bodycolour over graphite on paper by John Ruskin (1819-1900), who had a lifelong interest in architecture. This study of the cathedral is from the south-east side.

Flickering: William Holman Hunt (1827-1910) was a Pre-Raphaelite Brotherhood founding member. Outside of his (self-)portraits and landscapes, his work doesn't resonate as deeply with me as other Pre-Raphaelites'. This 1867 piece is particularly atmospheric.

The River Girl: John William Waterhouse's 1888 'The Lady of Shalott' oil on canvas is inspired by the end of Tennyson's 1832 poem of the same name. It features a woman only allowed to see the world reflected in a mirror. When she looks at Lancelot directly, the mirror cracks and she is cursed. Lying herself down in her boat, she drifts towards Camelot "chanting her deathsong".

Unstoppable: John Everett Millais (1829-96) painted 'Ophelia' in 1851-52. His 'Autumn Leaves' of 1855-56 is considered to mark the start of his move away from the Pre-Raphaelite style towards a new form of realism. This poem picks up too on the transience of youth and beauty (a common theme in his work). It imagines a contemporary autumn-leaf scene, the nature of inspiration and how this might be similar but also different now. This is written, like other poems here, keeping in mind some Pre-Raphaelite doctrines (nature, genuine ideas, heartfelt) and the brilliance of colour in many of their paintings.

Before something burns or bursts: 'Priestess of Delphi' is an 1891 oil on canvas by John Collier (1850-1934). The Oracle at Delphi (Pythia) was an initiated female priestess chosen to speak as a possessed medium for Apollo, the god of prophecy. In Greek mythology, laurel is Apollo's sacred tree. Bay leaves come from a laurel tree and are used as a spice in cooking.

Owerblawing: The 1903 oil on canvas 'The Shortening Winter's Day is Near a Close' (hung alongside Pre-Raphaelite art in the Lady Lever Art Gallery in Port Sunlight) is now attributed by the gallery website to David Farquharson (1839-1907), though it was previously attributed to Joseph Farquharson (1846-1935). Both were Scottish landscapists and 'owerblaw' is the Scottish word for 'to cover over or be covered with snow'.

Indigo Dreams Publishing Ltd
24, Forest Houses
Cookworthy Moor
Halwill
Beaworthy
Devon
EX21 5UU
www.indigodreamspublishing.com